I0504756

Sober To Drunk

Introduction:

Before I begin. I would like to mention that I don't promote or encourage any actions, words or ways of life mentioned in this book. This content might not be suitable for all readers, since I did not pre-plan the content of the book. Moreover, I will surly not be in a normal state of mind while writing. The last thing I would like to point out, is that I'm not an expert book writer. I don't have the knowledge on how to structure a short book. I'm just applying what I think a short book suppose to be.

Usually when I get tipsy and specially when I get drunk, many ideas, theories and realizations start rushing through my mind. I don't think I'm the only one who have experienced something similar to that. Thats why I decided to write this book to keep a written record of what will come to my mind in that mental state. Eventually, in the next day i will most probably forget those realizations and ideas wishing if only I had noted them down. I also want to share this experience with you in this short book, which I'm planning to write and finish it in half a day. Starting now. I urge you my dear reader to consider the same approach by reading the whole book in one session, so that you live and feel this experience with me. My estimation is that It will be done within 6 hours including the breaks which i will take in between. I will stop writing and call it a complete short book, whenever I get knocked out by alcohol or whenever I feel that I cannot process words anymore. The next day, I won't change anything I have written. I will just review to correct some spelling and grammatical mistakes. I will try my best since english is not my native language.

Phase 1 (Sober 101):

Currently, it's 5pm, Im sober and my beers are being chilled in the freezer. I think they'll be ready for consumption after 1 hour.
Only three beers, but very strong beer. Each can has 12% of alcohol.
The last meal I had was 4 hours ago, it indicates that I will have lower tolerance for alcohol. Im sitting on my bed facing down the laptop while writing. Taking a posture which i feel will cause me to get drunk much faster. I guess it's the result of low brain blood flow caused by my tilted neck. My room is quite small, almost shaped like a cubical.
It's about 168 square feet. It has a bed in the middle, wardrobe on the left side of the bed, small cabinet in the right side, a table on the corner left of the room and some boxes and bags on the right side which belongs to my Ex-girlfriend. I might mention her story later on.
Maybe not, but who knows? I will be drunk. No. She is not the reason why am drinking. I almost forgot about her existence.
Not completely, since some of her memories are still in my room.
Hopefully one day I will find a way to send them back to her.
She lives in a different country than mine. Im Sorry, but for political reasons I cannot disclose this information. This is the only thing that I cannot reveal. Once again, who knows? My mind will be out of control and I might mention it. I assure you that i will write down all my thoughts and will never amend them. Even if they are very personal.
As mentioned earlier I have three beers on the freezer.
I might have an extra beer, but I will try to avoid doing so, since it might cause a hangover the next day.

This paragraph is being written twenty minutes after the previous one.
I got interrupted by a phone call from a friend, an Ex-colleague to be exact. He contacted me yesterday via WhatsApp. Asking the usual question. "how are you?". We haven't had any sort of communication for almost one year. We used to be colleagues working in the same department, but in different professions.
Back then i used to work for a company based almost 200 km from my hometown. After I left the company two years ago, we still kept in touch

for a while. Mainly because he needed my experience and consultation. He got lucky and was hired in another company located in his hometown, but in a different position than his previous one. In fact, his new position is similar to the one I used to occupy. Due to his lack of experience in that field, he used to contact me regularly to help and aid him with his work. When he reached to me yesterday via whatsApp. I felt that he only reached me just to ask some questions regarding work. Today's call has proven me right. In his call, he asked me about something which his company needs to implement and which I have already implemented before in our previous company.

After that he told me about some new job openings. I interrupted him politely and told him that I'm no longer seeking for a job.

To justify my stand on why I'm no longer searching for a job, I told him about a bad interview experience which I went through lately.

I also explained to him my take on the situation with hiring nowadays. In short I said the following:

"I will not get a job unless I embrace the simple saying, (scratch my back and I will scratch yours)".

With my last sentence and after saying goodbye, we ended the call. Due to the economical changes and levels of maturity the country is going through. The "Scratching" mentality was introduce, which is.

*"Mr. Jasco. Of course you are aware that companies are trying to cut costs. It's no longer the same as before. Many employees were terminated and removed to reduce the cost. Only the most competent and others who have formed a tribal group will be able to stay. If you can help adding value to our tribe and enhance its power. Then congratulations. If I'm going to be benefited personally by you, for example sexually, then you are welcome. Otherwise if you are going to be a threat and I might lose my job or my promotional opportunity, then it's better to avoid hiring you" . - **inside the mind of an interviewee.***
It's a long subject which I will not touch for now. However, I have already

started writing another book about my experiences with the interviews I had during the last two years. In that book, I made a comparison between the interviews I had prior to my hirings and the recent interviews. I had attended several interviews after my resignation. After my third interview, I realized that I don't want to go through this tedious waste of time experiences. I meant by that, is going through the unprofessional work environment and the hiring cycle as a whole. In fact, it's one of the reasons I resigned and decided to aid and work for myself. Don't we all feel the same. I decided to attend other interviews just for the sake of writing a book on that subject. One time I attended an interview while being tipsy. Another time I acted like a fool. I even pretended that am super nervous in a way I was kicking the table while talking. I did all that just to see the reaction of the interviewee and what's the real intension behind the interview. Allow me to explain. In some cases I noticed that they had already chosen someone to fill that position, but they needed to go along with interviewing candidates just to silence internal auditors. Again, It's a long subject which I will hopefully tackle in another book.

During my career path. I have occupied many positions, within two different establishments. The first one was related to rescue and fire fighting. I shuffled between three different departments during my six years in that organization. I forgot to mention that I had a police training for 6 months before joining. The first occupation was somehow a secretary position for the branch officer. I saw the officer for the first time only after six months of me joining. During this six months there was no substitute for him. As far as I know. He broke one of his legs while playing soccer, thus he needed a medical leave to heal from that injury. When he rejoined after his medical leave, he was assigned for a training course for another two months, then I think he took a normal leave. I guess. I don't remember. Anyway I had two colleagues working with me. One of them was very obese. He was born like that. The building had one floor. Ground for fire fighters and trucks, while the first floor had offices which were abandoned and empty. Total wreckage.

Some of the empty offices were a sanctuary for birds, since there were no windows. The reason is that the building used to be the main headquarter. Then another bigger headquarters was built in a different area. Eventually, all clerical and administrative staff moved to the new building. Our floor had only two functional and clean offices, which are linked together but separated by a door. One of them was for the three of us and the other was the officer's. Due to his absence and since his office was bigger, we always used to sit in his office to chat, drink tea and coffee and have breakfast there. Ah, I almost forgot about the old cunning office boy from East Asia. One time I wanted to pull a prank on him and he ended up in the hospital. It was mainly his fault. I'd rather not not telling that story, but back then we had minimum work to do. The three of us were responsible for handling the administrative work for the staff working in the branch, such as applying leaves, printing letters, attendance, roster management and updating their data. In addition to taking care of the branch needs in general, like reporting vehicles malfunctions, requesting for parts, inks, food supply etc. Back in the days there was no automation on the system and things needed to be done manually. I also Forgot to mention that my work place was 5 minutes drive from my home. Another fun fact is that currently the building exists no more, since it was demolished and a new one was built but in a different location. What I've learned from one of my Ex-colleagues there, is that automation was finally implemented two years after my resignation. Few of my Ex-colleagues are still my friends until this day. One of the two mentioned earlier was my only friend back then. Even when we moved to the main headquarter, we were still working together and kept our friendship. We used to hangout almost daily. Nowadays I have almost no friends and even no best friend. I lied. I think I consider my Ex-wife as a best friend somehow. I guess. Im still in touch with her. Not physically of course. For the record, she is from the same country as my Ex-girlfriend.
Now It's 6:30 pm. I was defrosting a chicken before I started writing. I will have to clean it by using salt, lemon, vinegar and ginger powder. Then I'll leave it for 30 minutes. After that I will marinate it using different

types of spices. A method I learnt from another Ex-colleague who is still working in the previous company I used to work for. The one I left two years ago. He was a dear friend. I can even say that my friendship with him was similar to the one I had mentioned in the previous paragraph. No. Not My ex-wife, but the other guy who I used to hangout with. I had many experiences with him. Because the company was located 200km away from my hometown, I used to be his roommate for a period of time. Both friendships with him and the other guy reached to a point of just saying "Hi" from time to time and being virtual friends on social media. Excuse me. I will start cleaning the chicken. After I come back I will stop writing about my previous work experiences and open a new different subject. Whatever subject comes to my mind at the time.

Phase 2 (Sobriety):

Hi again. I just finished cleaning the chicken. It took me almost 10 minutes. Good news. I just opened my first beer. Im having some spicy snacks. I think it's from India. Found it today when I was at the grocery store. The best was to give you a clear picture of what my beer and snacks looks like, is to show you the real picture.
Im sorry to inform you that I cannot show the pictures.
At first I blurred the companies names and logos from the pictures. Searching Google. I wasn't able to know if I could use pictures of trademarked products. To avoid legality issues and to not promote drinking, smoking and bad eating habits. I decided not to include the images. If you are wondering why I kept this part in the book instead of removing it. Simply because as I stated in the introduction., that the premise of the book is to write down whatever comes to my mind. Moreover and as promised, I will not remove any part later on. This will add authenticity to the concept. I really wanted to show the pictures :(
I am a chain smoker. Disclaimer once again. Im not encouraging this act, but am just being honest and it's for the sake of "authenticity".
I already smoked almost 4 cigarets since I started writing till this point. Im starting to feel the blood pressure on my neck due to of my posture. Usually on this time of the day I will be trying to write down ideas for

books, sketches, movies or editing videos. I have some followings on social media around 80k in total. Yesterday I uploaded two different videos. One on my youtube channel and the other was on my instagram account. Both received good interactions and reviews. I've created those accounts as a hobby, but am trying to use my followings for self promotion in the future. For example to promote this short book. The idea of the video which I have uploaded yesterday on youtube is the following. In that video I recorded myself whispering on the mic, mocking the ASMR trend. If you don't know what is ASMR then please go ahead, search for it and brace yourself for an internet weird phenomena. Im not judging the people who make such videos nor the viewers. Personally, I just don't understand what's the point of watching someone whispering in order to relax or feel sleepy. I think it's a type of a new fetish.

Allow me to elaborate further. In my video I whisper for about 5 minutes as if am being serious. In my speech i asked the viewers to send me requests for role-play ideas that I will partake in. I have also updated the viewers on my future video uploads, where I will be recording myself eating big amounts of weird food while combining it with ASMR, where a mic will be up close my mouth, so you hear every single bite.

Actually it's another bizarre existing trend called Mukbang. Speaking of that, few days ago I watched a video of a lady performing Mukbang on a whole barbecued crocodile.Coming back to my video, I then requested the viewers to send me money so that I film myself while spending it on behalf of them. I ended up the video by saying:

 "send me your love ones and in my next upload I will film myself while making love to them".

To make it short for you, i ended the video by giving the following advice: *"Enjoy your life with your family and loved ones. Use your own eyes, minds and reactions, instead of watching your favourite YouTuber's reactions on a certain video or content. Eat and enjoy the food using your mouths not others mouthes. Long story short. Watch (the content) of your favourite celebrity ,Youtuber or influencer not their daily life."*

Combining seriousness and the silliness, the viewer will start to understand my sarcasm on these tends. If you are already aware of most Youtube content and the current online trends, then you will understand where i'm coming from.

I'm about to finish my first beer. My back and neck will explode from pain. Sorry but I will take a break then resume writing.

Phase 3 (Euphoria aka Tipsiness):

Alright I took a five minutes break. It's not easy writing a book while drinking in this posture. Before we move to the next subject I want to wrap up the previous one. What I want to say is that we really. I mean I think that. You know what? I'm really stuck. I really don't remember what I wanted to say. I think alcohol is kicking in. I will light me a cigarette. During the five minutes break I took while laying down on my bed. I watched my subscription feed on youtube. I came across a new upload from a christian truther channel. For the record I don't believe in religions and am not a conspiracy theory believer. I respect all faiths and beliefs. The reason why I watch such videos and other contrary videos. Is for me to know and understand different ideologies and views. At the end I will form my own opinion on that matter. I only watched the first minute of the mentioned video. It was about some news outlet covering the conspiracy theory of Chemtrails. I don't think I will continue watching the rest of that video later on. Usually I do watch full videos from that channel, but I found the conspiracy of Chemtrails quite generic. What I mean by that is....

Before I proceed explaining. You need first to have some background on this conspiracy. So if you don't know what is Chemtrails, then please read about it, so that you can digest my take on this concept.

I feel that you are saying to yourself:

"I wasted my money on this book, until now I don't know what the hell this drunk non-English writer is talking about. Even Google cannot ease my process of understanding him". If that's the case then am sorry for you loss. At least look at the bright side. You helped a broken drunk

person financially. You spent some free time knowing a little bit about another person from another part of the world, which is me. Most importantly. And most importantly. I really forgot what I was suppose to say regarding the bright side of buying my book. Anyway. I still remember what I wanted to say in regards of Chemtrails. I have mentioned that its a generic conspiracy theory.

What I mean by that is, if governments really want to poison and depopulate us, then they don't have to do it by using Chemtrailing. We are already far away from a healthy natural life. The nearest example is me. I'm currently smoking, drinking, eating some packed snacks containing chemicals and reverence. My neck is bent while writing on a laptop. The room air is cold because of an AC generated by chemicals. Im receiving radiations from my laptop, the smart phone next to me and the wifi connecting these devices. Oh one more thing. The chicken which I'm planning to eat was produced in an artificial farm. It was cleaned and will be marinated by spices and liquids which are made by chemicals. The oven is electric. So why should governments invest and be so eager to use Chemtrails to kill us?

I think people are already contaminated in away that, wherever they go, they are leaving chemical trails behind them.

Here is briefly my whole take on conspiracy theories in general.

Yes I do believe that there are few people who are controlling the world due to the evil powers they possess. They want to reserve this power to themselves and few selective elites. They don't want to share their pieces of the cake, yet. Side note. It's the first time I use the word (yet). Anyways. Yet they allow certain people to have wealth, fame, fortune and whatever the latter desire in order to help and support those elite to be able to sustain and continue being in control. One conspiracy theory suggests that those people chosen by the elite, have to sell their souls to the devil. Well, I believe that devils, angles and god have no existence as individual beings rather that spiritual construct of physical individuals. Any of these physical individuals can hold devilish, godly or angelic energy thus, to me selling your soul to the devil means that you are embracing a devilish spirit by indulging in evil unnatural, non-angelic and ungodly actions and behaviours. Some other conspiracies claim that you have to become gay, bisexual or be used sexually in order to advance and reach to a certain level in life. Well its not about sexuality, but the idea that you are forcing yourself into something which is against your believes and principles. With your own well, you are allowing others to take part of your given godly freedom. It's an unnatural and evil thing to do to yourself. Once you agree to partake in that, then you are sucked into a swirl of evil. Your wishes will be granted not because of your hard work or creativity but because you cheated your way to reach to the levels you don't deserve. In addition to that, you will be eliminating the chances of the talented, creative and hardworking people who were suppose to be in your position. Whatever I've just mentioned briefly is a metaphor of (selling your soul to the devil). I just realized two things:

1- In order for me to find a job i need to sell my soul to the devil.
2- The interviewee who earlier gave us his internal thoughts is gay.

You will have to excuse me while I marinate the chicken and grab the second beer. I already finished the first one.

Phase 4 (Excitement):
Wow I can't believe its 8 pm already. Just finished marinating the chicken. I will post the picture right away since I own the copyright. Unless the chicken sues me. If you have a weak stomach or if you are a vegan, then please skip to the next page. I'm not a good photographer.

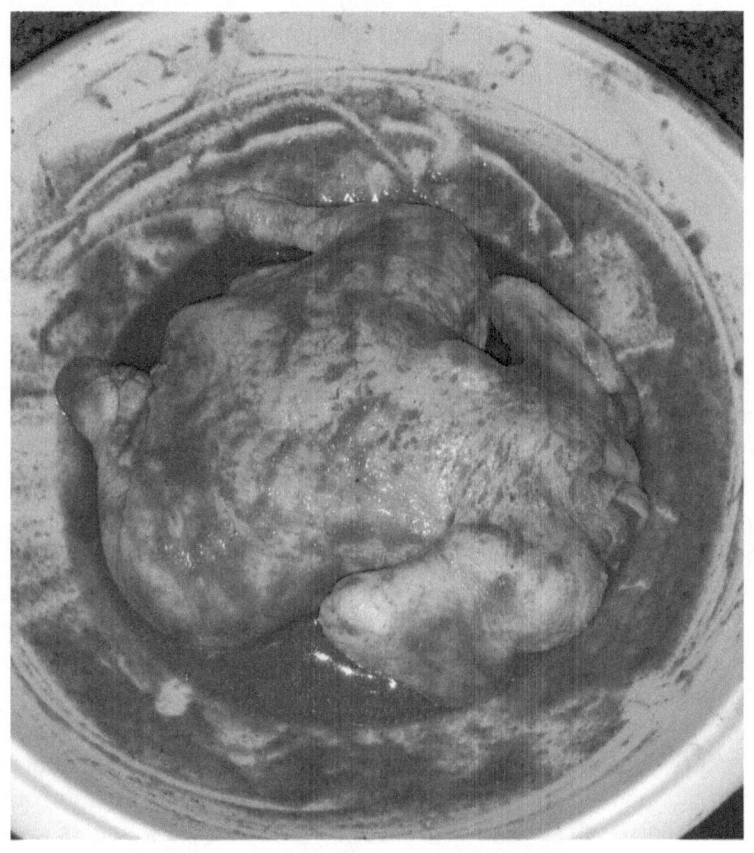

Let's resume. At the moment, I'm smoking and enjoying my second beer. Whats next ? What should I write about? Honestly I have no idea. It took me about two minutes of thinking, then I decided to write more about myself. Truly I feel that I'm not sitting alone by myself. Moreover, I can feel your physical presence in my room. Don't be scared I'm not that creepy. It's a great feeling knowing that you are currently reading my book. Thank you for giving me such an overwhelming feeling. It's also weird since we don't know each others name, face, identity etc. Are you a he, a she or a them. I used (them) pronoun to reference gender fluid people. Previously while writing, I tried intentionally to avoid expressing my ideas and views on gender vs. sexuality. I remember that during one of the topics discussed, I have briefly mentioned something related to sexuality. To be honest I was about to give my opinion on that, then preferred not to do it. It's a very sensitive subject and very difficult to cover without receiving backlash. Why not discuss it? I have no idea why I avoided that before. So here is my take on that subject. I mentioned earlier that anyone can be angelic, demonic or godly.
To me, any natural behavior is considered as angelic. Going against nature is defiantly not godly either. I was an alcoholic during a period of my life, then I became sober, then alcoholic once again, then sober. Currently I'm an alcoholic. Being so means that I have adopted an unnatural behavior. Therefore, for you to reach to this point of the book, I congratulate you. We have the same spirituality.
Is it a bad thing ? Maybe not. It might give us some experience to share with others. To me that's the ultimate human revolution. It's not about biological change rather than the spiritual side of it. I want to point out that the definition of spirit or soul according to me is the thoughts or cognitive thinking someone possess in his/her/they mind. I was not talking about the traditional concept of a soul which inhabits the body. Im aware that I'm not the only one who believe so. This belief was passed to me directly or indirectly by another human being and this is what I call the human evolution.
Excuse me while i visit the toilet because the alcohol inside me made an evolution and turned into something I need to get rid off.

<u>Sober To Drunk</u>

Welcome back. After sending the new evolved beer into a pipe trip, i had to spray perfumes on the hallway leading to my room due to the strong cigarets smell. I live with my brother and father but my room is in an isolated part of the house separated by a hallway. Sometimes they walk across the hallway to reach to the kitchen. Rarely they do so. Just in case if it happens, then by camouflaging the smokes with perfumes, I'm respecting their smelling senses and hiding the fact that I'm a smoker. My father is a smoker himself and non of my 4 brothers are. They don't know if I'm a smoker or not, but am sure they feel that I am. I don't want to talk about my family since I'm not a family guy. Im not talking about the TV show (Family Guy). Ok let's change it by saying I'm not a family person. Long story short. Yes I do live with my brother and father, but I haven't spoken to my father since almost 2 years, even though I see him sometimes when I leave or enter the house. As for my brother, only 8 meters is separating my room from his. However it was almost 4 months since I had a face to face conversation with him .We do communicate from week to week via WhatsApp, we even send each other voice notes and that's all. I would like to highlight something to you my great reader in case you were wondering. You might think it's strange that I live in my father's house with my brother and I might be a teenager or younger. Nope. In my country, it is very normal to have such kind of setup. Im 34 years old. In fact my birthday was 4 days ago. My brother is 36 years old and my father is in his eighties, I guess.
After the last sentence. I stopped writing for about 10 minutes because of another phone call. I usually will get one phone call in a month. It's so weird that the day i decided to write this book I have received two phone calls. Usually it's not the case. This phone call was from my father's secretary. My father runs a private business providing maids and house cleaners. Who has called me was the secretary of that business. We did have some few exchanges before on issues related to the office PC which she needed me to fix. Six months ago she had blocked me from her phone. Why? Because one time I got drunk. Wait. Hold on. Let me give you another important piece of information before I explain why she did block me. The secretary and some of the

maids are living in same compound in where I live. But in a different house. The compound is surrounded with huge brick wall. Inside that wall are three houses. A house occupied by me, my brother and father. The second is occupied by my eldest brother, his wife and kid. The third is where the secretary and some of the maids are living in. Let's come back to the reason why she had blocked me. One night I got too much drunk from consuming brandy. I decided that I needed company. Eventually, I contacted her via WhatsApp. I just noticed that I have used the word (WhatsApp) a lot in my writing. It's Like they are desperate for an alcoholic marketing campaign. Strangely, (campaign) has a similar pronounce to the word (champagne). This book reeks with alcohol smell. Apologies for leaving the topic. I sent her a message asking her to come to my room. It was 11 pm. Usually both my father and brother sleep at this time. Father is retired since 20 years and brother will be working the next day. Anyways she came to my room. I started talking to her about my father and the business. Bla Bla Bla. I thank her for the room company, she leaves and I sleep. The next night I got drunk once again. Thinking of what happened the night before that. I started admiring the slick ways I used to persuade her into being in my room, talking, sitting next to each other. Even thought she was risking her job for this bold move. I felt superior. I could ask her to come and give me a massage or maybe we have sex. To me she is below my league. Im not a womanizer. I don't care about women appearances rather than the personality. So personality wise she is 4 according to my standards. It will be very difficult to engage with her into any physical actions even if she had an appearance of 10 out 10. But I was drunk. I sent her a message asking to come once again. At the beginning she hesitated. Feeling that I'm losing control and my superiority. I went and stood in front of her house door. Then sent a message informing her that I'm already here. She opened the door, quickly and quietly took me inside before someone sees us. All I remember that night is that her room was cold and dark. Her daughter was sleeping on the bed not aware of my existence. That night, I was in a drunk stage which I rarely reach. I felt am outside the universe, among the starts. The room was very dark I could barley see her face. I remember asking her the big question. Is your daughter actually my sister? Until now I cannot recall her answer. There is a rumor circling around between my brothers and sisters stating that her daughter might be our sibling. She has similar face features. The kid regularly visit my father. I can hear them when he plays with her in the living room. Either because he is the father or he is a pedophile. Of course Im joking he is not. I knew about the rumor after I had an exchange with my sister regarding the subject. One time my sister approached me for assistance, as everybody does. After helping her I indirectly plugged in my own conspiracy theory which she had confirmed. Anyway me being drunk I started kissing her and end up giving her oral sex. I forgot to mention that she had a husband who was visiting her from time to time. I even asked her about the strength of the relationship. Clearly is was shaky since I just pleasured her. That old cheating woman. When I get drunk I usually try to be philosophical and ask people questions about their personal lives in order to guide them to a better one. The moment I asked her about the husband, she gave me an expression that indicated repulsiveness and disgust towards the so called husband. Now I remember why I did ask her about the husband. Actually I have another theory that after my father knocked her out. He had to bring a stunt double to act as the kid's father. From her expression I understood that he is a tool to convince us that she is indeed married and the kid is her daughter from him. When I licked her pussy. My tongue told me that she was very wet and her pussy was tight. This piece of information backups the theory of the stunt double. It means that she is not having enough sex. It also can indicate that the husband is inactive sexually. Ironically I couldn't get an erection to penetrate her. Drunk or not, I was easily getting erections and having sex not that am old or unexperienced. Maybe I couldn't because I realized that she might be my step mom. I asked her to do the penetration part tomorrow during day time. I returned back to my room and slept. The next day she sent me a romantic picture via WhatsApp. I hated myself and felt disgusted. A normal feeling since I was sober. Upset from my actions and manipulations. Feeling filthy for even having a personal conversation with her. I couldn't believe that I kissed her and gave her oral sex. It seems that my penis had a mind of its own and wanted me to stop this charade.

I don't blame my lips or my tongue. Both were in the front lines receiving alcohol shots. I simply replied to her by sending *"Im Sorry"*.

She blocked Immediately knowing that I was only interested in her because I was drunk. I forgot to mention that when I was in her room she told me that she was attracted to me but was afraid to approach me and didn't know how to do so. Figures. Even my family are intimidated by me. I went against them when I got married to my Ex-wife before asking for their approval. It's a big deal in our culture. I only gave them the news after 4 months of getting married. I could see the anger in their faces, but no one has confronted me or said anything about it. I got some calls during that time from my siblings pretending to ask about me in general, but I felt the calls' true intensions were to open that subject and talk about my marriage. They tried indirectly during the phone calls to mention it. I was certain that it was the only reason for calling me.

No one calls me or contacts me just to say hi. Specially my family. Im an outcast. People only reach to me just when they need help. That's actually what happened when the secretary unblocked me and decided to call me 40 minutes ago. Without detailing the conversation. She needed me to help her with the office's internet bills and to give her the password of the wifi in our house. At First she sent me a message asking to see me in person to talk about something. I insisted not to do so by sending her the following *"tomorrow we will discuss"*.

Then she decided to call. I wanted to skip seeing her for two reasons:

1- I'm already drunk.
2- I want to be able to finish this book experience successfully.
3- Im enjoying your company my dear reader.

Allow me to take this quick toilet break.

Phase 5 (Confusion):

Welcome back. I just opened the third can of beer because I can. Got it? The beer is too cold and a bit icy. I think I will go with a 4th beer. As mentioned I want to avoid the fourth one because I need to wake up tomorrow at least at 11am. I need to renew my car registration. It's a long and interesting story. To make it short, I was suppose to renew it a month ago but I had another car under my name. That car is being used by a driver for a shop in which I used to be a partner in. According to our traffic law. All fines must be paid for both vehicles before being able to renew the registration of any. There are some fines that even if paid, it will result in the impoundment of the vehicle for certain amount of days determined by the severity of the traffic fines committed. The wonderful lovely shop driver have committed many traffic fines that resulted in the impoundment of the shop's car for 28 days. There is another option which is to buy the impoundment. Each day costs 27$.

27$ x 28 days = 756$.

I'm happy that I still can use numbers and the calculator although of feeling very drunk. My Ex-partner in the shop will handle paying the fines. I just realized that I have many Ex's. If I keep adopting this way of life then I will surly have an Ex-life. It even rhymes with Ex-wife. Anyway, I could've asked my Ex-partner to pay for buying the car's impoundment since its not my problem, but it was big amount. Plus I barely use my car. It's not even his fault. The terminated driver made those fines. Last month when my car registration was due. I have paid for all my fines, insurance and car inspection fees. Upon trying to renew the car online, the system informed me that I cannot proceed due to the unpaid fines of the shop's car, even if paid, it must be impound. Thats why tomorrow I need to visit the traffic department since today is the last day of impoundment. Moreover, tomorrow will be the last day for vehicle inspection certificate and insurance validity. In regards to the shop story and why I was forced to leave the partnership and why the car is still under my name. It was because both my father and my Ex-wife. Wait please, before touching this subject I would like windup the previous by saying.

Sober To Drunk

For me to agree on the impoundment of the shop's car instead of asking my Ex-partner to buy it, was indeed a ridiculous move from my side. You know why ? I left the shop influenced by my Ex-wife and father. I haven't spoken to my Ex-partner for almost for 4 years .Then I suddenly I appeared in his life after I resigned and divorced my wife. You know what? I apologize, but I decided not to write about this subject. What you need to know is that before 11 am I need to be awake, so that I can renew my car registration. If it will not happen tomorrow, then after tomorrow will a weekend and I will end up paying 70$ extra. It will also cost me two hours extra from my time to finish some processes which I've already made one month ago. Why? Because in 2019 almost 2020 automation still sucks ASS. Im not even going to edit or delete this part of the book. Im drunk, I don't care. I'm torturing myself for the sake of this stupid idea of a book. Yes am mean and devilish spirited. I decided to drink just to write this book and receive some cash. Im giving you and myself hard times just for 2$. You know what? I will increase the price. Wait. I just received a message from my Ex-wife. Wait please she is still sending me. Please allow me to read them then I will get back to you. Im back. She asked me how many views on average I get from my Instagram account. I told her almost 20k. She said thanks. I think she wants to help me financially. I'm not doing that good. That's why am writing this book which am grateful because you decided to purchase and read. Im using 11pt as font size. I think I will increase it so that I can publish it as an Ebook. I wanted to mention that I still support my Ex-wife financially. You might ask me the following question. How come you left your job two years ago and still have an income. Well its because of the left overs I still have from that shop. Remember when we spoke about the car? I also have lended people some money during the past years which I had to beg to get it back in order to survive. Funny. When they need money, they become so angelic and down to earth. When it's time to return that money, they step on you like a sadistic king. Never lend anyone your money. Never never. I learned a painful lesson. I also make few earnings from my freelance work like writing books, youtube, social media and online miscellaneous activities.

In general. Thank you for purchasing the book, it really means a lot to me. Im very tired and drunk. I need to windup writing this book. I meant to say this short book. I still have some energy left on me. I will spend it all because of your support. You can contact me using the following email : ....
Ask me about anything. I think I will not cook the chicken tonight, and I will not drink another beer. Once I finish my car renewal tomorrow, I will review whatever I wrote for proofing, then I will put my final words before I publish it. Despite the book being short, I'm actually 6.2 feet tall.
I feel that I cannot write anymore. Maybe I'll be able to continue after resting or I'll just call it a day. In this case thank you for your time and goodbye.

Sober To Drunk

It's not over yet. I still have energy to write more specially after I took a 10 minutes break. Right now the time is 10pm. I started writing at 5pm. In the beginning of the book I have estimated that it will take me at least six hours to finish this book. You know what? Fuck the six hours rule. I just decided now to complete the book at 12 pm. New rule. The Seven hours rule. Unscripted unplanned as usual.

I just used one of the empty beer cans to urinate. No time to be wasted using toilets. I'm waiting for the secretary to call me because I need her so bad right now. You already have an idea about my financial situation. Please support me. You know what ? don't support me. I will really feel ashamed tomorrow. Im really having a strong back and nick pain because of writing while drinking. That's it I cannot take it anymore.

I swear its a nightmare. It was a bad idea from my side. I don't think I will consume more beers. I will end the book right now and lower its price. As promised, tomorrow I'll review and edit the book only for grammatical and spelling mistakes, without removing anything which has been written. Not that I will do a great job. I even don't know why I decided to write in a language which is not my native. Yes I will have to edit it as I mentioned earlier, but will not delete whatever I wrote. Take care and thanks a lot.

Sober To Drunk

After another 10 minutes break I realized that I promised to continue writing this books until 12am. It's 10:20 pm right now. Never drink alone and never drink regularly. Its better to drink only on celebratory occasions and within a company. However, you can still drink alone only if you had a good rest in that day and you had a good meal before drinking. Make sure you have snacks. Alcohol is filling your stomach with poison. Definitely you don't want poison to eat your insides. Snacks and food will be good to distract alcohol away from your internal organs.
Im still waiting the secretary. Right now I'm very passionate. If she does contact me then that's it. I decided to make love to her. At this point, I don't give a damn about the circumstances of doing so. My penetration will be latex free. Sexual transmitted diseases? We are going to die one day. Pregnancy ? So what ? I know how to cause natural miscarriage. It's not like I haven't done it before. Don't worry. I will update you tomorrow when I write the book's conclusion. I just remembered that I did meet the her three times before. One time was in my room and two times in her room while her daughter was sleeping. The Second time I made out with her and played with her big boobs. The third time I gave her some licking between he thighs. She is suppose to be home. Why is she taking more time? Maybe she knows that I will attack her romantically so she is getting prepared?
I just was interrupt by my best friend which is my Ex-wife. She sent me a vague question once again regarding my followers on social media. Fuck them I'm not giving them any of my content today. Only you my reader. You deserves my content tonight. Yes, only you my lovely reader. This might end up as a book or as an Ebook, who knows? I'm trying my chances. By the way I decided to provide the screen shots of my conversation with my Ex, in case you thought am hallucinating.
I guess better not share. I don't have her consent.
Damn its 10:40 pm. I cannot take it any longer. I thought I can sustain more. Yes I did believe so, but according to the way am sitting and writing, its drunk invoking even without alcohol.

Phase 6 (Entering Stupor):

My eyes just landed on an application icon in my toolbar. I downloaded it two days ago. It's called blender. A tool for creating 3D models and Animations. Back in the day I dabbled with different developing tools. Programming, animations, 2d , 3d, photoshop…etc. Nowadays I became less creative than I used to be. I just use the right tools and link them to the best resources available. I'm not a creative nor intelligent. Just an intermediary, connecting people with ideas, connecting ideas with ideas, connecting people with people, connecting videos with videos and so on. Im a glue and that's it. By glue, I didn't mean my sperm which I will inject on the secretary tonight. Im only a connector. Some of you guys are creative, talented and great. You don't want someone like me telling you what to do. COME ON. Be energetic do your thing. Fuck the system and fuck whoever is telling you that you can't do it. Look at me for example. Im a washed up, drunk, wannabe writer, bullshitter who wasted your valuable time and money. Im not proud of that and I do apologize. Don't waste your life like I did. If you have a dream then study it , plan it and achieve it. Don't let anything stop you. Oh he his unworthy, oh he is just coping so and so, oh Im afraid of people's reactions. If you like something then you will find someone who will like it as well. Just take the action and don't hesitate. You will lose nothing. Plus it will help you to enhance and add more to your craft in the future. You don't need a person like me telling you so and so. Be godly and be certain that whatever you do, you will receive a positive acceptance. It created a backlash? So what? Keep doing what you think is right and what you believe in. I'm not a fool preacher who tries to put you down. Just be courageous and fuck the world. Everyone has potentials and abilities. A person became successful only because that person took an action and decided to (do it), while the rest decided to be neutral. he, she or them took an action while you stayed motionless. Please allow me to take a small break, it 11 pm already. One hour remains to reach to the seven hours goal. I got encouraged by my own motivational words.

During my 10 minutes break. The secretary finally appeared. She sent me a message asking for the home wifi password. I replayed back. It seemed that she was able to connect, expressed by the thumbs up emoji. "Is it a good connection?" I asked.
Still no replies from her side. Why wouldn't she ignore me? This sums up my life experiences with people. They take what they want from me then ignore and try to avoid when I'm in need. It's 11:15pm, until now i have completed 6 hours of writing including the breaks. Unfortunately I think the (six hours rule) rules. It was a good ride, thank you for participating and have a good life. See you in the next one.

Phase 7 (Stupor unedited):

Hold on. iM still awake. Dubbed indirectly by the secretary. Wait. You know what the security has called me complaining about the wifi coverage. I went outside to show her that I bought a wife extender which is making the house wifi wifi better. It costs me 25$. When she had difficulties connecting to home wifi I asked her where we can plug my extender as a test. She pointed out the location and her phone signal was working as a charm. I asked her to give me 25$ so that i buy another one for your small house. She started to look around for money. I interrupted her by saying tomorrow I will go to renew my car then I will pass to your office to by the extender for you. Of course after I take from her. As I said I think my writing is a mess but anyways we agreed on the terms and condition. Am happy because its 11:45 pm already and I was able some how to sustain myself to write until this time. This secretary adventure gave me adrenaline specially when she was shushing me , telling me that my father might hear our conversation. I told her don't worry I've long time here to know when he does sleep, wake up or be in the house. The chicken is in the oven. im having my fourth beer since 20 minutes ago. I already consumed the quarter . If you are wondering its 500ml. It is still 11:50am. Am not planning to cheat the system. I have 10 minutes with you gays to give you my last words. I swear to god I never planned this. In fact its a mess what I'm tying but tomorrow I will rectify it.you know I just stopped for 2 minutes after my last sentence because I forgot what I need to say. It took me another two minutes to say…. Just be honest, just be yourself , just trust yourself be your fucking self. Do whatever you think Is right what relieve you and suits you but in humane and ethical way. 12 pm already I did reach my goal. What about you ? What the fuck I just wrote to you ? I decided not to eat the chicken toady I just remembered that I saw the secretary daughter . I need her mom sexually and I need to kiss the kid as sibling love. Never drink alcohol and stay away from it/. You know why because I'm using using you right now o get my money. You dm food .am a fool am sorry I swear I'm drunk. I will try to slep by by.

My Last words:

Whatever you are reading now is being written after two days from the last phase. The next day, the alarm woke me up at 9:30 am.
I remembered that I needed to visit the traffic police for my car registration. I also remembered that there was a cooked chicken in oven which I needed to put in the fridge. I cannot recall the details of what I wrote but I knew that I did write something. Usually having such nights cause me to forget many of these details. What's funny is that I made my precautions by adding notes to my alarm so that I don't forget what I'm suppose to do the next day. I ended up remembering everything except the fact that I wrote these alarm notes.

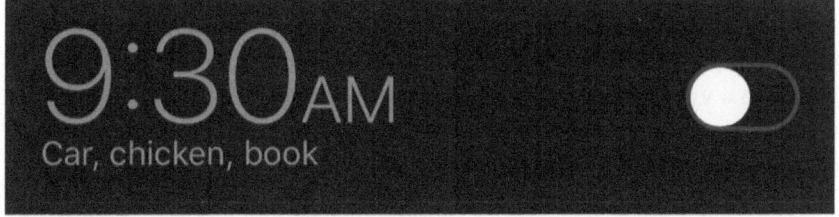

No hangover, but I was laying down on the bed browsing the internet until finally I had the power to standup, take a shower, dress up and leave my house only at 11:20 am. I was not successful renewing the car. I spent almost 2 hours in the traffic department due to system issues thus, I will have to go through the processes and pay for the insurance and car inception certificate validity after two days. When I returned back home. I tried to review and edit the book, but my energy and mood was not that productive due to the drinking on the night before. I was able to produces some content to my online followers which was simple and not that creative. Images and book phases were added just now during the revision. Fun fact, that night during my writing, I was capturing my mental state on a separate piece of paper so that I can add the proper headline and section to each section of the book.
I found today a website containing medical alcohol intoxication stages. I applied the same stages according to what I have noted down.

The results were unbelievably very matching. I will add the link to the website and the stages at the end of the book.

After reviewing and editing I only removed my email address. This was the only thing I changed. Other than that all what you have read was what I wrote that time without any amendments. I kept the last phase unedited in order to show you the raw material. It was also the best representation of my mental state at that point. Indeed I feel ashamed of myself. People who know me will feel even more disgusted when they read this book. Deep inside I felt I need to document this experience so that I feel bad about my alcohol consumption. Im happy to announce that it did really help me. I don't feel like drinking. In fact I did not drink the day after that night. We could all see how messed up I was. Revealing personal details. Hurting and using others. Feeling careless, lifeless and angry. Being selfish and insulting people. There was a part in phase 4 which sounded like insist due to incoherent linking of narratives. I kept this part on purpose to show you how a drunk person start mumbling and jumping from one story to another creating confusion and misunderstanding. In general such mental state will cause you a lot in terms of health, family, relationships, productivity, self-esteem and more. Im sure that you have made other observations and conclusions. That was one of the main purposes of making this short book. If you never drank alcohol then you have this book as a sample. If you do drink alcohol then control it. If you are an alcoholic then be sure that one day you will end up embracing yourself like I did.

Upcoming books:
- Millennials Short Stories - Miscellaneous *Stories.*
- Marrying a job - *Short Book*
- The Book of no author - *Novel*
- Six nights with the devil - *Novel*

<u>Sober To Drunk</u>

Below are the seven stages of alcohol intoxication I based the phases of my book on. Thank god I did not reach to the last two stages.
Taken from the following link: <u>healthline.com</u>

1. Sobriety or low-level intoxication
A person is sober or low-level intoxicated if they have consumed one or fewer alcoholic drinks per hour. At this stage, a person should feel like their normal self.
BAC: 0.01–0.05 percent

2. Euphoria
A person will enter the euphoric stage of intoxication after consuming 2 to 3 drinks as a man or 1 to 2 drinks as a woman, in an hour. This is the tipsy stage. You might feel more confident and chatty. You might have a slower reaction time and lowered inhibitions.
BAC: 0.03–0.12 percent
A BAC of 0.08 is the legal limit of intoxication in the United States. A person can be arrested if they are found driving with a BAC above this limit.

3. Excitement
At this stage, a man might have consumed 3 to 5 drinks, and a woman 2 to 4 drinks, in an hour:
- You might become emotionally unstable and get easily excited or saddened.
- You might lose your coordination and have trouble making judgment calls and remembering things.
- You might have blurry vision and lose your balance.
- You may also feel tired or drowsy.

At this stage, you are "drunk."
BAC: 0.09–0.25 percent

4. Confusion
Consuming more than 5 drinks per hour for a man or more than 4 drinks per hour for a woman can lead to the confusion stage of intoxication:
- You might have emotional outbursts and a major loss of coordination.
- It might be hard to stand and walk.
- You may be very confused about what's going on.
- You might "black out" without losing consciousness, or fade in and out of consciousness.
- You may not be able to feel pain, which puts you at risk of injury.

BAC: 0.18–0.30 percent

5. Stupor
At this stage, you will no longer respond to what's happening around or to you. You won't be able to stand or walk. You may also pass out or lose control of your bodily functions. You may have seizures and blue-tinged or pale skin.
You will not be able to breathe normally, and your gag reflex won't work correctly. This can be dangerous — even fatal — if you choke on your vomit or become critically injured. These are signs that you need immediate medical attention.
BAC: 0.25–0.4 percent

6. Coma
Your body functions will slow so much that you will fall into a coma, putting you at risk of death. Emergency medical attention is critical at this stage.
BAC: 0.35–0.45 percent

7. Death
At a BAC of 0.45 or above, you are likely to die from alcohol intoxication. Excessive alcohol use causes approximately 88,000 deaths annually Trusted Source in the United States, according to the Centers for Disease Control and Prevention (CDC).

www.ingramcontent.com/pod-product-compliance
Lightning Source LLC
Chambersburg PA
CBHW031509210526
45463CB00003B/1144